Senses

Written by
William Anthony

North American adaptation copyright © 2025 by North Star Editions, Mendota Heights, MN 55120. All rights reserved. No part of this book may be reproduced or utilized in any form or by any means without written permission from the publisher.
Senses © 2021 BookLife Publishing
This edition is published by arrangement with BookLife Publishing

sales@northstareditions.com | 888-417-0195

Library of Congress Control Number:
The Library of Congress Control Number is available on the Library of Congress website.

ISBN
979-8-89359-292-4 (library bound)
979-8-89359-297-9 (paperback)
979-8-89359-306-8 (epub)
979-8-89359-302-0 (hosted ebook)

Printed in the United States of America
Mankato, MN

012025

Written by:
William Anthony
Edited by:
Robin Twiddy
Designed by:
Amy Li

All facts, statistics, web addresses and URLs in this book were verified as valid and accurate at time of writing. No responsibility for any changes to external websites or references can be accepted by either the author or publisher.

Photo Credits

Images are courtesy of Shutterstock.com. With thanks to Getty Images, Thinkstock Photo, and iStockphoto.

Recurring images – Micra (brain, sunburst pattern), Lorelyn Medina (children vectors), illustrator096 (clouds). Cover–p1 – KittyVector, Beskva Ekaterina, Inspiring, Oxy_gen, svtdesign, p2–3 – Samuel Borges Photography, Kitty Vector, Oxy_gen, p4–5 – Africa Studio, svtdesign, LuckyVector, Toey Toey, Inspiring, p6–7 – govindamadhava108, Mila Ma, Pogorelova Olga, Studio Barcelona, p8–9 – Panda Vector, ilikestudio, Studio_G, Gaidamashchuk, p10–11 – Faberr Ink, Anatolir, svtdesign, Perfect Vectors, p12–13 – Infinity, Olga Shlyakhtina, Seika Chujo, p14–15 – Inspiring, Pro Symbols, Kolpakova Daria, Alexander Lysenko, p16–17 – Ksusha Dusmikeeva, Rido, Alexander Lysenko, p18–19 – Rudmer Zwerver, TY Lim, Sko Helen, p20–21 – 32 pixels, Alexander Lysenko, Lukiyanova Natalia frenta, p22–23 – goodluz, ANURAK PONGPATIMET, p24 – Inspiring.

Contents

Page 4	The World Around Us
Page 6	Sniff, Sniff
Page 8	Ear to Hear
Page 10	Eye, Eye, Captain
Page 12	Yum, Yum
Page 14	Touchy Feely
Page 16	Senses at School
Page 18	Be Like a Bat
Page 20	Superhero Senses
Page 22	A World of Senses
Page 24	Glossary and Index

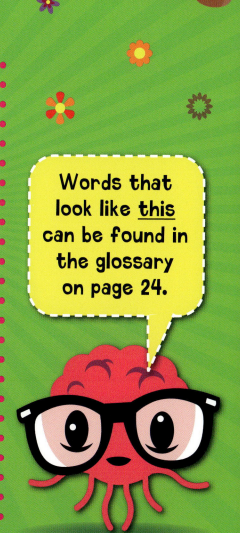

Words that look like <u>this</u> can be found in the glossary on page 24.

We use senses to understand the world around us. We have five main senses. They are smelling, hearing, seeing, tasting, and touching.

Sniff, Sniff

We use our noses to sniff and smell things. Some things smell nice, but other things might stink!

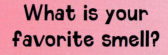

What is your favorite smell?

Let's find something to smell. Take a walk outside. Can you find a flower or a pretty leaf? Hold it to your nose and …

Ready, Set … SMELL!

What did it smell like? Was it nice or not?

Ear to Hear

We use our ears to hear different sounds around us. The sounds go into our ears and bounce off our eardrums.

Your eardrum is inside your ear, but never try to touch it.

Let's test out different sounds. Grab a pencil and some different objects. Tap your pencil on each one to see how it sounds. On your marks …

Eye, Eye, Captain

When you look around, you are using your eyes to see. You see an object because light has bounced off it and into your eyes.

Light

It is difficult to see in the dark. Try it for yourself! Find a room, close the curtains, then turn the lights off …

Yum, Yum

You can taste things using your tongue. Your tongue has lots of <u>taste buds</u> on it. Taste buds help you find out whether food is sweet, <u>sour</u>, or something else.

What is your favorite flavor? Mine is raspberry!

Let's do a taste test! Grab two pieces of fruit, such as a strawberry and a lemon. Taste both and try to say how they are different. Do you have your fruit?

Touchy Feely

Touch is how we feel things. Our skin is very <u>sensitive</u>. It can tell us how something feels.

We can feel things with lots of different parts of the body.

Let's test out our touch. Look around the room. Try to find:

- Something soft
- Something hard
- Something rough
- Something smooth
- Something warm
- Something cold

Ready, Set ... TOUCH!

Senses at School

We use our senses all the time. We use them at home, at the park, at school, and everywhere we go.

What do you use your senses for at school? Make a list of everything you might use your senses for.

Use this example to get you started.

Ready, Set ... LIST!

Smell	New books
Hear	Teacher
See	Table
Taste	Lunch
Touch	Pencil

Be Like a Bat

Some animals have amazing senses. Did you know that bats have incredible hearing? They use their hearing to find out where things are in the dark.

Let's try being like a bat!

Find an adult to help you. Close your eyes so you cannot see, and let your adult guide you into a room. Use your senses such as touching, hearing, and smelling to figure out where you are.

Ready, Set... EXPLORE!

Superhero Senses

Have you ever wanted to be a superhero? Lots of superheroes have super senses. Draw yourself as a superhero with a super sense.

What is your super sense? Can you write a sentence about it?

Which super sense did you choose? Can you see through walls or see in the dark? Can you hear things from very far away? What about smelling danger?

A World of Senses

Some people cannot use all their senses. People who are blind find it difficult to see. They might have a guide dog to help them get around.

People who are deaf find it difficult to hear. Some deaf people might use a hearing aid. It helps them hear the world around them.

People who are _disabled_ use all sorts of things to help them sense the world.

Glossary

disabled	limited in doing certain things because of a medical condition
eardrums	the parts of ears that vibrate when sounds hit them
sensitive	quick to figure out how something feels
sour	a strong, sharp taste
taste buds	the small spots on your tongue that let you taste things

Index

animals, 18
disabilities, 22–23
hearing, 5, 8, 17–19, 21, 23
school, 16–17

seeing, 5, 9–11, 17, 19, 21–2
smelling, 5–7, 17, 19, 21
tasting, 5, 12–13
touching, 5, 8, 14–15, 17, 19